First World War
and Army of Occupation
War Diary
France, Belgium and Germany

40 DIVISION
120 Infantry Brigade
King's Own Scottish Borderers
10th Battalion
10 June 1918 - 28 February 1919

WO95/2611/4

The Naval & Military Press Ltd
www.nmarchive.com
Published in association with The National Archives

Published by

The Naval & Military Press Ltd

Unit 10 Ridgewood Industrial Park,

Uckfield, East Sussex,

TN22 5QE England

Tel: +44 (0) 1825 749494

www.naval-military-press.com

www.nmarchive.com

This diary has been reprinted in facsimile from the original. Any imperfections are inevitably reproduced and the quality may fall short of modern type and cartographic standards.

© **Crown Copyright**
Images reproduced by permission of The National Archives, London, England, 2015.

Contents

Document type	Place/Title	Date From	Date To
Heading	WO95/2611/4.		
Heading	40th Division 120th Infy Bde 10th Bn King's Own Scoth Bdrs Jun 1918-Feb 1919 Formed 1918 June.		
War Diary	Etaples	10/06/1918	10/06/1918
War Diary	Buysscheure	10/06/1918	23/06/1918
War Diary	La Belle Hotesse	23/06/1918	03/07/1918
War Diary	W Hazebrouck Line	03/07/1918	04/07/1918
War Diary	W Hazebrouck	05/07/1918	07/07/1918
War Diary	Mill Fontaine	08/07/1918	08/07/1918
War Diary	Moulin Fontaine	09/07/1918	09/07/1918
War Diary	West Hazebrouck	10/07/1918	10/07/1918
War Diary	Moulin Fontaine	11/07/1918	15/07/1918
War Diary	West Hazebrouck	15/07/1918	18/07/1918
War Diary	Moulin Fontaine	19/07/1918	31/07/1918
War Diary	La Belle Hotesse.	01/08/1918	06/08/1918
War Diary	Lumbres.	07/08/1918	09/08/1918
Miscellaneous	Programme No.1.		
War Diary	Lumbres.	10/08/1918	12/08/1918
War Diary	Le Noir From	13/08/1918	13/08/1918
War Diary	A La Promenade	14/08/1918	19/08/1918
War Diary	In the Line	20/08/1918	29/08/1918
War Diary	Eeckhout Casteel	30/08/1918	11/09/1918
War Diary	Le Grand Beaumart.	12/09/1918	16/09/1918
War Diary	Sheet 36A. 1/20,000.	17/09/1918	30/09/1918
War Diary	Sheet 36 Ned 1/20000 Grand Beaumarghe	01/10/1918	01/10/1918
War Diary	Equinghem	02/10/1918	06/10/1918
War Diary	Sheet 36 NW 1/20,000	06/10/1918	13/10/1918
War Diary	Pont de Nieppe	14/10/1918	15/10/1918
War Diary	Sheet 36 1/40000	16/10/1918	19/10/1918
War Diary	St Andre	20/10/1918	27/10/1918
War Diary	Sheet 37. 1/40000	28/10/1918	28/10/1918
War Diary	Lannoy	29/10/1918	06/11/1918
War Diary	Leers Nord	07/11/1918	09/11/1918
War Diary	Pecq	10/11/1918	10/11/1918
War Diary	Herinnes	11/11/1918	12/11/1918
War Diary	Toufflers	13/11/1918	23/11/1918
War Diary	Herinnes	24/11/1918	30/11/1918
War Diary	Toufflers	01/12/1918	28/02/1919

WO 95/26111/4

40TH DIVISION
120TH INFY BDE

10TH BN KING'S OWN SCOTH BDRS
JUN, 1918-FEB 1919

Formed 1918 June

170/40
Army Form C. 2118.

JUNE, 1918.
VOLUME I
10th K.O.S. Borderers

WAR DIARY
INTELLIGENCE SUMMARY.
(Erase heading not required)

Instructions regarding War Diaries and Intelligence Summaries are contained in F. S. Regs., Part II. and the Staff Manual respectively. Title pages will be prepared in manuscript.

Place	Date	Hour	Summary of Events and Information	Remarks and references to Appendices
ETAPLES			The C.O. 2nd in command Adjutant Transport Officer Quarter master and H.Q. coy of 100. N.C.Os and men of this new Battalion. (10th Garrison Bn)	
ETAPLES	10.6.18	7.23 am	detrained at ETAPLES 2.30 a.m. and marched to BOISSCHEURE, where the Batt. was to be organized. The march of about 10 kilometres was accomplished without anyone falling out, which was considered very fair, with few exceptions. nearly all (all carried full pack, ground sheets and blankets) Kitbrench ration was carried	
BUYSSCHEURE	10.6.18	8.30	arrived BUYSSCHEURE	
"	11.6.18	11.30	Reinforcements arrived by Majr E.F.O.P amounting on strength apn 900 other ranks. The Coys were made up strength Majr E.F.O.P amd 1914 equipment H.Q NORT.D.M.F Coy. Capt L J MORGAN E. Coy. Capt L.C.CARPENTER 869 H.R Capt. W.C.GLOVER P.Coy and nine Subaltern Officers	
"			Ratting and organising Battalion OR all being fixed with 1914 equipment appearing in clothing etc completed. (1 Batt H.G named by officers) Lt Col M ARCHER-SHEE D.S.O 2nd in command Major S. Boyle M.C. Adjt Lieut W.M. CLARK LIEUT Q.M. GREENHALGH. TRANSPORT OFFICER CAPT. L. TRITTON. MEDICAL OFFICER. LIEUT. CALDWELL. R.A.M.C.	O.R
"	13/6/18		Training – coy drill, 2nd and Platoon drill Revielle at 6 am. Breakfast 7-30, Specialists. S.B.R drill Revielle 6 am Breakfast 7.30, Specialists courses were organized L.G. Bombing Physical training and musketry carried on by competent instructors coy 4 nights	
"	3/6/ 4		Training – any of the above went route marching	

SHEET (2)

Army Form C. 2118.

JUNE, 1918
VOLUME I

WAR DIARY
or
INTELLIGENCE SUMMARY.
(Erase heading not required.)

10th Garr. Bn. K.O. Sc. Bord.

Place	Date	Hour	Summary of Events and Information	Remarks and references to Appendices
Boyschoeque	15/6/18		Ch. Army Authority sanctioned that 130 other ranks of German Battalion be to trained as the 10th General Regt. Kilty Burn Section Bearers.	9/R
"	"		Training carried on with Coy arrangements. Rifle range the same Post held by the H.Q. instruction, grenade firing Bay and Platoon Constructor 6 per Establishment. Great trouble in Bomb	
"	"		The Battalion was inspected by B.D.C. Lt. Col. Dixon M.C. Genl. J. Ponsonby C.C.M.G. D.S.O. the afternoon. He expressed himself very pleased with the appearance of the men.	9/R
"	16/6/18		The C.O. and 2nd in Command and by Bay Commanders reconnoitred the WHAZEBROUCK LINE in the LA ROMARIN (AREA) 40th Div. transferred to XV CORPS	
"	"		Training — experience such as out-posts, piling rifles Lecture by Commdg Officer on Germany and German War Aims	
	19/6/18		Battalion inspected by D.A.G. The general expressed himself well pleased with the men	9/R
	20/6/18		Env. Gs. N.C.O. inspected all S.B.R. and found them in a satisfactory condition. Training carried on as usual, under Bn/Coy N.C.O.	9/R
	21/6/18		The Batt. football match money prize given by Comdg Officer	9/R
	22/6/18		Orders received that Battalion would move to BELLE EGLISE (M.28.B)	9/R

WAR DIARY or INTELLIGENCE SUMMARY

Army Form C. 2118.

JUNE 1918
VOLUME I
10th Garr[ison] Bn. K.O.S.B. (Bordon)

Place	Date	Hour	Summary of Events and Information	Remarks and references to Appendices
BUYSCHEURE	22/6/18	8 am	Troops moved off independently from billeting areas & were marching order (Wardrobes were transported to LA BELLE HOTESSE by M.T. Officer) N.C.Os and men embarked at a point on the BROXEELE—ST MOMELIN ROAD arriving at LA BELLE HOTESSE about 3 P.M. Tents and Bivouacs	O.T.R.
LA BELLE HOTESSE	23/6/18	3 P.M.	were drawn from 30 Inf. Bdge dumps and moved to Bere	O.T.R.
LA BELLE HOTESSE	9 a.m.		The Battalion was inspected by the Inspector of Medical Services detail.	
	24/6/18		40 O.R. were transferred from Jan Bn and transferred to Labour Companies. The Bn moving as per programme all boys have found employment at the L.a Belle Hotesse Camp	O.T.R.
	25/6/18		Applications for jobs and Papers arrived at 35 sp on the L. Belle Hosp Camp.	
			On the whole the pastures were very satisfactory.	
			Training of Specialists also carried on. Lewis Gun and General Musketry. Lecture lessons in Gas & work carried on	
	26/6/18		Unstriped. Lectures and Practice for Officers, N.C.Os and men.	O.T.R.
			Bath manner the W.H.Z.E Branch M.G. & transfer to General Officer Commanding 120th Inf Bdge inspected the dispositions	
	27/6/18		The Commanders Officers and Coy Commanders with N.C.Os made a Reconnaissance	O.T.R.

JUNE 1918.
VOLUME I
10th Garr Bn. K.O.S.B.

WAR DIARY

INTELLIGENCE SUMMARY

Army Form C. 2118.

Place	Date	Hour	Summary of Events and Information	Remarks and references to Appendices
LA BELLE HOTESSE		3.20	A Battalion rectum or W. HAZEBROUCK arrived. Thereafter an ordinary Coy and squad drill S.B.P. drill P.T. as per programme	
"	29/6/18	1.30	10 new officers arrived from the SCOTTISH DEPOT CALAIS all have been in FRANCE with the exception of 2nd/Lieut RICHMOND 5 Res Bn K.O.S.B. J.R.	
ditto	30/6/18		Training under Coy arrangements. Lethal schemes Bathing, Lectures on Coy P.T. Scouts and sniper above all. bathing by motor lorries on p.92 P.T. Lect under/Lieut Jordan for instructions in numbers parade daily Lewis Gunners averages was 2 over all coys and umpires leading section for instructions men and officers were detailed to Coys and taken on strength of Battalion football matches arranged and recreational training	

Walter W Roberts Lt
A/Capt for Lt Col
Officer Comdg. 10th Bn K.O.S.B.

July 1918
Volume II
Copy 10 4 B 2 K D S B

WAR DIARY
INTELLIGENCE SUMMARY.
(Erase heading not required.)

Army Form C. 2118.

Place	Date 1918	Hour	Summary of Events and Information	Remarks and references to Appendices
LABELLE HOTESSE	1 July		Courses for Specialists. Training as per programme by Commanders carried out. Tactical schemes by Coys.	War
		2 P.m.	Battalion paraded (en masse) practised Royal salute marched passed in Column. (all available Officers NCOs and men were present)	War
	2nd July	3.40	Battalion was ordered to parade as part of the 36th Inf Bdge at a point on the 1/20,000 S 36 A ROMAINE ROAD. The Battalion paraded on that parade ground marched C 10 A 9.9	War
		3.15	at 2.30 p.m in column of route arrived at inspection parade ground at Bonpensier	
		4.15	Bdge was formed up by Battalions in close column of Companies. Inspected by H.R.H. The DUKE of CONNAUGHT who expressed great satisfaction	War
		5 p.m	at the appearance of the Bdge. Parade moved off independently by Batt to their respective billeting areas.	War
	2 July	7.30	(Training tactics P.T etc) Orders received from Bdge that Batt would move supped branches in W HAZEBROUCK line for 4 days from the 3rd July to 7 July carrying out trench routine as provided in front system trenches (patrolling feeling of sentries) preparations will made for the projected move, brevet line reconnoitred by Officers before proceeding orders issued by C.O. of the move at 7.30 pm	War

2S
7 sheets

PAGE 26

Army Form C. 2118.

WAR DIARY
or
INTELLIGENCE SUMMARY.

(Erase heading not required.)

July Volume II 10th I.O.S.B.

Place	Date	Hour	Summary of Events and Information	Remarks and references to Appendices
LA BELLE HOTESSE	3 July		Leaving in the morning the Boys moved off independently to their positions in W. HAZEBROUCK LINE (9 nos. battle order and all men fully equipped). When in the trenches 2 Coys dug and repaired trenches and 2 Coys carry on with specialists classes (training generally) a range has been made which will enable Coys to carry on musketry practices during tour of trenches	2 PM first Coy moved off. WHR WHR
W HAZEBROUCK LINE	3 July 4 PM		duty) occupied sector of W. HAZEBROUCK LINE. Trench routine carried out.	WHR
W HAZEBROUCK LINE	4 July	9 a.m.	O & P Coy detailed as working parties under 145 & 6° R.E. at Gand Isnard dump paraded in Drill order with haversack ration	WHR
"		8 a.m.	F Coy on the range till 11 a.m. E Company training as per programme	
"		11-2	E Company on range Rapid Practice Trench routine carried out Sentries posted at 6 p.m. on every post all condite. is carried out equipment is worn by front line Coys during trench training hours. Coy practice patrolling by night between the hours of 10 and 2 p.m. Sentries are not posted after midnight except when considered necessary	
"	4 July		All boys stand to at 4 a.m. & 4.30 a.m. Rifle inspection carried out regularly Section orders were issued by Comdg Officer, O & P Coys	WHR

Army Form C. 2118.

1/6 K.O.S.B.

WAR DIARY
INTELLIGENCE SUMMARY.
(Erase heading not required.)

July 1918
Volume II

Place	Date	Hour	Summary of Events and Information	Remarks and references to Appendices
W HAZEBROUCK	5 July		The relief was carried out at 6 p.m. The code word "Edinburgh" was sent to B H Q. on the relief being complete. Draft from Reinforcement arrived 4/9 O.R. all Category B.I. B mm	W rue
"	6.7.18		Two boys worked on trucks of W HAZEBROUCK line. 2 Companies carried training as per programme, course for specialists were carried on as usual. Specialists musketry on range and bathing	W rue
"	7.7.18		The b/50 boys on training the previous day, work under R.E. on trenches, the other b/50 training as per programme.	
		3.45	Batt. moved out of trenches\ Lens of July having been completed and marched down to Devious area.	W rue
MILL FONTAINE	8.7.18	9 am	Batt. was inspected by Major General Sir W.E. Peyton KCB KCVO DSO. The Bn was drawn up in close column of Coys. He then inspected Coys at training, outpost schemes. P.T. musketry and rapid fire at the LA BELLE HOTESSE range. At 10.30 he inspected On Transport, remainder of day carried out by Coys in training as per programme.	W rue

WAR DIARY
or
INTELLIGENCE SUMMARY

(Erase heading not required.)

Army Form C. 2118.

10th K.O.S.B.

July 1918
Volume II

Place	Date	Hour	Summary of Events and Information	Remarks and references to Appendices
Roukin Fontaine	9/7/18	Morning	Training Physical, B.F. etc. New Lewis Gun Classes commenced. Scouts, Snipers & Bombers.	
		Afternoon	Bomb classes. Officers & Signallers attend Pigeon lecture by Signalling Officer. Stretcher Bearers attend lecture by Medical Officer.	wue
West Hazebrouck	10/7/18	Morning	Tactical training by Battalion of WEST HAZEBROUCK line. Companies were in position by 10 a.m. and inspected by G.O.C. Lewis guns & 66,000 S.A.A. taken up by Transport. Dinners cooked in trenches. Battalion returned to camp by Companies and arrived back between 3-30 & 5-30.	wue
Roukin Fontaine	11/7/18	Morning	Training Physical & B.F. Drill etc. for "E & O" Coys. L.G.P inoculated.	
		Afternoon	Recreational training for "E & O" Coys. 3 Battalion Football match.	wue
do	12/7/18	Morning	"E & O" Coys Physical, Bayonet Bayonga etc. L & P. days not for inoculation	
		Afternoon	"E & O" Coys Training, Bay Drill etc. Snipers & Scouts classes	
do	13/7/18	Morning	Training Physical Range etc. Bathed & Companies whole Battn attends	
		Afternoon	Recreational training	
do	14.7.18		Church Parades C of E, Presb, & United Board & Wesleyan Service in Camp. R.C. voluntary service at Beaucu	wue

PAGE 5

Army Form C. 2118.

WAR DIARY
or
INTELLIGENCE SUMMARY.

July 1918   10th K.O.S.B.   Volume II

(Erase heading not required.)

Instructions regarding War Diaries and Intelligence Summaries are contained in F. S. Regs., Part II. and the Staff Manual respectively. Title pages will be prepared in manuscript.

Place	Date	Hour	Summary of Events and Information	Remarks and references to Appendices
Moulin Fontaine	15/7/18	Morning	Training. Platoon Drill P.T. & L.T. Bombing & Lewis Gun Classes	wwe
Out Skylebrick	"	Afternoon	Proceeded to Lunches West Skylebrick line in Position 4–10 pm	
do	16/7/18	morning	two Companies working under C.R.E. 15th Corps other two Companies Lunch	wwe
"	"	Afternoon	Contd. During the night two bombs dropped close to Batt. HQ. wounding the C.R.	
do	17/7/18	morning	two Companies working to C.R.E. 15th Corps other two Companies	wwe
"	"	Afternoon	Trench Routine	
do	18/7/18	morning	Two Companies working under C.R.E. 15th Corps other two Companies trench routine	wwe
"	"	Afternoon	W. Batt. Relieved to Camp Moulin Fontaine at 3pm 3.15pm 3.30pm & 3pm T.O.	
Moulin Fontaine	19/7/18	morning	Major F. Doyle M.C. assumes Command of the Battn vice Lt Col. McArdee-Blee D.S.O. M.P. to Command Brigade	wwe
"	"	Afternoon	Training Platoon Drill P.T. & Lewis Gun Scouts and Snipers Classes	
"	"	"	C of Drill & disposal of Coy Comdrs. all Brigadick Classes as morning	
do	20/7/18	morning	Training Extended Order & Platoons in attack etc also Baths & Range.	wwe
"	"	Afternoon	3 Ball football match	
do	21/7/18		Divisional Parade for C.of E. with arms Inspection by D.nl Comdr. & Deputy Asst Chaplain General, Crahy Luther Board Wesleyan Service in Camp Voluntary Service for C of E & Presn.	wwe

PAGE 6

July 1918
Volume II

WAR DIARY
or
INTELLIGENCE SUMMARY.

Army Form C. 2118.
10th K.O.S.B.

Place	Date	Hour	Summary of Events and Information	Remarks and references to Appendices
Moulvidaudure	22/7/18	Morning	Training Physical, Box Resp, Platoon Drill etc also Range.	nil
		Afternoon	Bomb throwing + Range	nil
do	23/7/18	Morning	Training P.T. & B.Y. & at disposal of Coy Cdrs also Lewis Guns Bombing + Signalling Classes	nil
		Afternoon	Practising Platoons in attack	nil
do	24/7/18	Morning	Training Assault Course + Range also Lewis Gun + Signalling Classes	nil
		Afternoon	Recreational training	nil
do	25/7/18	Morning	Manned WEST HAZEBROUCK LINE for instructional purposes and 1st Coy returned at 2.15 pm last Coy	nil
		Afternoon	returned 2.30. Work carried out training in assembling and briefs duty.	nil
do	26/7/18	Morning	Coy carried out training as per programme, Platoons in attack P.T. B.F. under B" Cmdrs.	nil
		Afternoon	P.Coy outpost scheme. ⅔ward onmoving practice. Ceremonial Drill	nil
do	27/7/18	Morning	Bn halted at LE ROMARIN Training as per programme Inter Competition announced	nil
			(attached Proposed Scheme)	
do	28/7/18	Sunday	Divine Service C of E, R.C. & O.field 11 A.M. Pres. Wesleyan United Board H.Q field 9-15 AM	nil
			R C at Berous 10. A.M.	nil
do	29/7/18	Morning	F & P Coys carried out first part of Inter Platoon Competition.	nil
		Afternoon	Reeves O.E. Corps General training as per programme. Lectures by Coy Cmdrs on men showing good "Esprit de Corps"	nil

Army Form C. 2118.

WAR DIARY
or
INTELLIGENCE SUMMARY.
(Erase heading not required.)

July 1918   10th K.O.S.B.
Volume II

Instructions regarding War Diaries and Intelligence Summaries are contained in F. S. Regs., Part II. and the Staff Manual respectively. Title pages will be prepared in manuscript.

Place	Date	Hour	Summary of Events and Information	Remarks and references to Appendices
Moulin Lestaine	30/7/18	Morning Afternoon	Major Gen Sir W Peyton KCB KCVO DSO Comdg XV Corps inspected the Batt on its leaving grounds during the morning. Attacks in programme of work carried out.	wre
Do.	31/7/18	Morning Afternoon	RFC & Continued. Inter Platoon Competition E & B Coys having ceremonial Drill "C" Coy Baths Guard Mounting Platoon & Squad Drill "O" & "D" Relieve on Outpost by Coy Comdr "O" Coy Baths	wre

SSMajor
Comdg. 10th Bn
The Kings Own Scottish Borderers

WAR DIARY
INTELLIGENCE SUMMARY

Army Form C. 2118.

August 1918
Volume III
10.16.0.a./13.

Place	Date	Hour	Summary of Events and Information	Remarks and references to Appendices
LA BELLEHOTESSE.	1/8/18	morning	E & F Coys Platoons in attack, who on arms take each. Lecture by Coy Officer.	
		10-0AM	6 & 9 Coys. Pt & B.F. Drill with S.B.R.	V.R.3
		11.30AM	7 & 6 Coys commencing Drill	
		11.30AM	3rd Platoons Musketry Revision in B.F.Hqrs. F.Coy. Battery & S.B.R Drill. Gas Lecture	V.R
		12.15 PM	G & I Coys Platoons in attack, notes on enemy's tactics on some by Coy Officers. All coys to have demo Gas.	
		10.0AM	Oil Coys Platoons in attack	
		6.0PM	E Coy & Platoons bathing. F Coy back hand, Revisional Training. G&I Coys same as F Coy	
		3.0PM	B" Class Junior Gunners Bombers Signallers, Lewis Bn crews about 60 Schwol as usual	
			Lime has given classes for Platoon Officers every 2nd time weekly, Tuesdays & Fridays 3-4pm	V.R
	2/8/18	9.0AM	Batts at La Honcour all coys. Lewis Guns La Belle Hotesse Range 8 to 10-30PM	V.R
		1.0PM		
	2/8/18	9.30AM	E.F&G Coys Tactical Scheme, E&G Platoons Blue Force, F.Coy Red Force attacking from La Honcourt assisted by 2TMBs Culminating in Platoons on attack	
		9.30AM	O&I Coys Platoons in final Assault, Ceremonial Drill Lecture on Trench Warfare	
		11.0AM		
		9-30to 11.0AM		
		after noon	Ceremonial Drill Lecture on management Route marching. Special Reconnaissance	
	5/8/18 morning		E Co ceremonial & squad Drill, Platoons in final Assault. F.Coy. PT & B.F. S.B.R Extended order Drill. Platoons in attack. O Coy musketry armor Platoon Drill. Lecture Esprit de Corps. Bathing & squad Drill. I Coy musketry Extended order Drill, Platoons attack.	V.R
		afternoon	All Coys. Route march. Special classes as usual.	3 S. 9 mm

August 1918.
Volume III
1/6 K.O.Y.L.I.

WAR DIARY
INTELLIGENCE SUMMARY.

Army Form C. 2118.

Place	Date	Hour	Summary of Events and Information	Remarks and references to Appendices
LA BELLE HOTESSE	6/8/18	9-11.5AM	Battalion will parade by Coy under Coy F.O. as per Coy programme. School Numbers tomorrow 9 not to include men will parade at 9am at C.21.a 6.3. Coys march to assembly point 9.15am detailed in parties of 25 including 1 officer & N.C.O.s. Battn marching order B'k'ft in Packs. Stores 500 F.A.K.M. in Cookers with each Coy. Transport moves off 6-0am. Rations for consumption E.H. will be with K.M.	91R
Lindres	7/8/18	2-30pm 4-30pm	F Coy on Range firing. E Coy to supply 5 Off. & some 260s & 96 O.R.s for markers. Practice as per attached programme. No 1, 2 & 3 Lewis Gunners fire on mid. Coys. G.O.P. Coys interested Order Drill & musketry. (Programme No.1)	91R
	8/4/18	7am 12-0	E. & P. Coys will carry out the following practices 2,3,4,9:00pm programme. F.P. Coys will detail 3 officers and 1 H.Coy 1 O.H. to supervise on Butts. F Coy will detail 7 N.C.Os & 96 O.Rs as markers. 7 other ranks as Range Sentries. (Programme 1)	91R
		1-0 to 4-30pm	F Coy on Range. E Coy markering. F Coy on Range. E Coy marching. P. Coy on Range. O Coy musketry Practices to be carried out. 6,7,8 & 9 as per programme. 5 boxes of S.A.A. to be taken to Range. (Prog No.)	
	9/8/18	7am 1-30	E Coy will detail 1 Off & 2 N.C.Os & 96 O.Rs as markers & 3 O.Rs as Sentries. 6 O.s. P.O.P. Coys Casuals to fire with Coys. detail 12 Off. for Butts. Lombaux march to X Range as per programme (Prog No 2)	91R
			All companies fire as per programme	

WAR DIARY or INTELLIGENCE SUMMARY

Army Form C. 2118.

August 1918
Volume III

Place: Lumbres
Date: 9/8/18
Hour: 1.0 to 2.30pm

Scheme for Field practice on Range F. Coy advancing in the open in Artillery formation suddenly find they are being fired on by Enemy's Rifle & Machine gun fire. Distance about 1550 yds. Special Idea. 3 Platoons immediately extend for attack, no. 1 Platoon in support. The firing line will open on Enemy's position at 500 yds. from front Lewis gunners of Plats to neutralize enemy's fire. Covered by short Sectional Rushes to 400–500 yds on the right enemy's Machine gunners come into action while line is held up, Platoon in support to reinforce & advance continues until final assault position 200–100 yds.

Targets:– Enemy advance post consisting of 1 NCO 30 OR 200 yds behind represented by (No 3 silhouettes) the scenic on back of Butts. Representing machine gun position & sections of Rifle men little garrisons in shell hole will be represented by following plates. Fig 3 Silhouettes displayed from Butts. Screens not to be fired on. O. Coy will fire at 5. Off. 11 NCO & 50 ORs as entries also 6 ORs as sentries. E.Pl. boys invading the instruction while above scheme in progress. E. Coy next for Tactical Scheme.

Remarks: JR

August 1918
Volume IV
10.10.13

Page IV

Army Form C. 2118.

WAR DIARY
or
INTELLIGENCE SUMMARY.
(Erase heading not required.)

Instructions regarding War Diaries and Intelligence Summaries are contained in F. S. Regs., Part II. and the Staff Manual respectively. Title pages will be prepared in manuscript.

Place	Date	Hour		Dist. yds.	Rounds	Summary of Events and Information	Remarks and references to Appendices
Programme No.1							
Practice							
1			2nd Cl. Elementary (Bulls Eyes)	100	5	Instructions for courses of fire.	
2 Application			—do—	200	5	Lying with arm or rifle rest.	
						—do—	
3 Rapid			2nd Cl. figure	200	5	Lying Bayonets Fixed 30 secs allowed	
4 Slow			—do—	300	5	Lying	
5 Rapid			—do—	300	10	Lying Rifle unloaded & mag empty until target appears. Loading from Pocket by 5 Rds of firearms a minute allowed	
6 Slow			1st Cl. figure	500	5	Lying	
7 Rapid			—do—	500	5	Lying correct to shoes or sand bags representing knapsack or lying over them	
8 Rapid			2nd Cl. figure	300	15	Lying. Rifle to be loaded & rds in mag. before the target appears. Loading from Pocket by 5 rounds afterwards; minute allowed	
9 Slow			1st Cl. figure	500	5	Lying	
10 Rapid			—do—	500	5	Lying 30 secs allowed	
11 Slow			—do—	600	5	Lying testing over arm 9*	
Programme No. 2							
19 Snap shooting			Figure No 3 (Silhouette)	200	5	Lying. Target exposes 4 secs	
22 Rapid			2nd Cl. figure	300	15	Lying Rifle to be loaded 4 Rds in mag of def. target apprs. Loading from pouch by 5 Rds. 1 min allowed	
23 Slow			1st Cl. figure	500	5	Lying	
24 Rapid			—do—	500	5	Lying 30 secs. allowed	

August 1916
Woolacombe
10th K.R.R.B.

WAR DIARY
or
INTELLIGENCE SUMMARY.

Army Form C. 2118.

Page 5 V

Instructions regarding War Diaries and Intelligence Summaries are contained in F. S. Regs., Part II. and the Staff Manual respectively. Title pages will be prepared in manuscript.

(Erase heading not required.)

Place	Date	Hour	Summary of Events and Information	Remarks and references to Appendices
Woolacombe	10/8/16	9.0 am S/d.D	E & O personnel of Bay on X Range, P & y & pericol 10ff spells & 96.10 as members.	
			3 ORs as orderlies. E & O boys will collect & Off exit to exposures in Butts & exposures on X	JTR
			Range as per programme.	
Slow	2nd Class 7if		400 yds 5 Rds - Lying Taking 5 snap Blank stones or sandbags & being exposed 1 sec	
			will arcs of fire uncovered	
Slow	300	5 -	Kneeling Taking snap on heads of figures & sereen	
			representing a wall & firing over the parapet.	
Rapid	300	15 -	Lying Rifle to be loaded & 4 Rds in mag after 1st of	
			objects heading from point by 5 Rds. 1 sec allowed	
			F E & O boys will fire together in groups on X range F a on empletion to	
			relieve P a in Butts	
		145 to 4.30 pm	Packers will be fed on Range Army Rifle Assoc Platoon Competition to be an accordance	
			with O.B 161/16/D Practice to be fired as ended	
			400 yds 5 Rds at disappearing target 6 secs exposure (silhouette No 5 Fig)	
			300 " 5 " Application 1st Class Figure	
			From 200 yds platoons will advance 200 yds firing rapid Bayonne targ. Charging	
			then getting into front spring 10 rounds rapid 2nd Class fig tgts as 200 silhouette	
			10 yards out to the main up platoons to fire as platoons 2 reps to fire at scene	
			Wire front practice by E & O Bays	

(A9129) Wt W358/P50 500,000 12/17 D.D. & L. Sch 52a. Forms/C2118/13

August 1918
Volume VI
Page 7

WAR DIARY or INTELLIGENCE SUMMARY

Army Form C. 2118.

Place	Date	Hour	Summary of Events and Information	Remarks and references to Appendices
Dumbrel	14/8/18	9.0 AM	E.F.O.Phoys will detail 1 O.H. to parcell fences. Gun teams to march to range under Lewis Gun Officer. Markers to be detailed from party going 9 am to	97R
		12.30	12-3 am at 200, 300 and 400 yds. Seven targets 50 men at 200 yds.	97R
	20/8/18	11.45 PM	Bn relieved by 13th G. Lancs & proceeded by train to La Suis Lines	97R
Choc Suis Lines	21/8/18	9 am	Bn paraded to relieve 9th R.S.R. Her in reserve at A.2 Promenade left L.S.L. Lines	97R
		9.30 AD	Destination reached 12.45 PM. Relief complete 3.0 PM. 13th Bn HQ established - Dw.1.8.8. Transport Lines D.19.C.1.2. Nothing received 12.0 PM. Light Shrav. taking place on sqt. Mersey autumn taken.	
A La Promenade			SOS signal received about 6-40am (Sector R.2) Bn stood to ready to meet on confirmation SOS cancelled 6-53 am.	97R
		10 am	Coys Harry Lys of pickets, Bullet shoots, kit with arms, Pt SB.R. Working parties found 30 ORs leading stores, Bonnaview Junnelary Coy, an Impression Dw.7.D. to ORs leading stores to 2.R.E. Coy. for Inversion Dw.7.d. S.S. Cornallis hl.	
	22/8/18	7.30 PM	10 ORs working in Sw. Canadian Lines by GM Marguarett Farm E.7.a. & 10 Obs at 1.0 PM., 13 ORs carrying H. Hollengate Dst.5.9, 10 ORs to 2 Rts boys at Brickstacks.	97R
			E20.c.7.0. 100 ORs Burying Cable South Bridge D.17.B. 85.90 100 ORs - ditto.	

August 1918
Volume III
10 Bn H.L.I.

Page VII Army Form C. 2118.

WAR DIARY
or
INTELLIGENCE SUMMARY.
(Erase heading not required.)

Place	Date	Hour	Summary of Events and Information	Remarks and references to Appendices
A La Pannerie	16/8/18			
	to 19/8/18		Same as for 15th. Specialist classes.	AIR
In the line	20/8/18		On evening of 20 Aug. Battalion was ordered to relieve 106 Batt'n of 22nd Div. in the line.	AIR
			F & W coys in position in front of La Couronne. E Coy but up position South of La Becque	AIR
			from E25c57 to E26c57. Remaining 2 coys were in reserve in wood between	
			Nollery Farm & Nobley Cottage.	
	21/8/18		On the morning of the 21st Aug. advanced Enemy attacked and repulsed its way shown	AIR
			to a line from New Cross E30d 6.0. F25c 8.6.	
	21/22/8/18		On night of this day Bn was ordered to extend its front Northwards taking over	AIR
			the line from 11th E.York's who held the front with 3 Coys in the line. E Coy was	
			then brought up to hold the line from Brake Farm L.S.T & joined up	
			with D Coy. C Coy in support parallel to main Road. Hoy Bears Becque	
			at about E23 c.9.0. During day of 22 Aug there was no movement.	
	22/23/8/18		On night of 22/23 a further relief was carried out. B Coy took over right half	AIR
			Post Borden to New Cross. Flag unsuccess'Roleceum E by neck stations to abley	
			Switch & B Coy took up position in trenches across Becque at E23 d.9.0.	

August 1918
Volume VIII   10th K.O.S.B.

WAR DIARY or INTELLIGENCE SUMMARY

Army Form C. 2118.

Place	Date	Hour	Summary of Events and Information	Remarks and references to Appendices
9th Fd Line	23/8/18		On 22nd Aug. C by was ordered to attack in conjunction with the 15th R.O.S.B. Later Bn boundary being Post Rouden a line drawn about L.k.73 there a line further drawn to a point about Y.a.k.9.9. They met with a heavy barrage machine gun fire. The whole of the line was not taking the Bn on the South being unable to get past the Louverlie. The line then ran F26c6.5 to I.k.73 thence to Rouen – Arches road. Casualties – 1 officer 2 ORs – killed – 16 other 19 ORs – wounded.	JR
			On night 23rd Aug another Coy was brought up to help hold the line. C by relief was placed to the Junth. C by waited from support near la Bacque.	JR
	25/8/18		On night of 25 Aug. C by was relieved by 6 by v E by withdrew to Cittry Switch. They were in R6a. Bn H.Q. moved into R.5a. e 6.	JR
	26/8/18		On night 26 Aug the Bn was taken over by 13th R.Innis. Fus. C & F boys remained in support in R.6a. on August M 27 Aug. C boy was withdrawn in F25a facing East.	JR
	27/8/18		On 8 27 Aug 13th R.Innis. Fus attacked across front in S E direction occupied line Bishops Court – Henne g.	JR

Page IX August 1918
Somme
II / 10th Bn K.O.Y.L.I

WAR DIARY
or
INTELLIGENCE SUMMARY
Army Form C. 2118.

Place	Date	Hour	Summary of Events and Information	Remarks and references to Appendices
	25/8/18		On night 25 Aug F Coy were relieved by Ebay in K6a. 11 Bavarians attacked in a SE direction & captured Bowery Cottages	03R
	29/8/18		and Rue Provost. On night of the 29th Bn was withdrawn into reserve at Les Anglais.	01R
			Total Casualties. 1 Officer Killed 1 wounded 5 O.Rs -do- 38 -do- 3 missing 32 sent Hospital sick Sick wastage of 11. sent Geo + 6 16/9/10/16	
FECK'HOUT CASTEEL	30/8/18		Battn moved to camp at CSCG 9.5. FECK-HOUT CASTEEL	01R
CASTEEL	31/8/18		Divine Service.	81R
			F Coy played P Coy football match resulted in a draw.	

J.W. Watson Lt. Col
Comdg 10th K.O.Y.L.I

WAR DIARY or INTELLIGENCE SUMMARY

Army Form C. 2118.

10th BATTALION, KING'S OWN SCOTTISH BORDERERS.

VOLUME IV Page 1

120
40

H.S.
3 attck

Place	Date	Hour	Summary of Events and Information	Remarks and references to Appendices
EECKHOUT CASTEEL.	1/18 10/18 11/18		Brigade in divisional Reserve. Battalion training.	G.T.R
	9/18 12/18		do.	G.T.R
LE GRAND BEAUMART.	9/18 13/18		Battalion relieved Rl. K.N. STAFFS in the line. Bn. H.Q. (temp) B28a49. Arrangements of Coys: BHQ B28d49. E Coy. Vicinity of Church at B28b1.4. F Coy. from B23a99 to B23d9-7. O Coy. B19.69.15. G Coy. from B23d07 to B28a64. (Sheet 36A 1/20,000)	G.T.R
	14/18		Quiet during the day. 77mm Gun active on NIEPPE SWITCH in vicinity of BHQ. Quiet before BHQ. Patrols & MG's active at night.	G.T.R
	15/18		BHQ at TAFFET FARM. B22C.H.9. Coy dispositions unaltered. Enemy shell active with 77 mm Gun. Situation unchanged. Patrols active.	
	16/18		BHQ shelled with 77mm shells. Machine Guns active on Enemy Posits and overhead MG positions during the early part of the evening. Patrols were sent out at 10pm to try & procure	G.T.R

WAR DIARY
INTELLIGENCE SUMMARY

Volume III
Page II

10th BATTALION, KING'S OWN SCOTTISH BORDERERS.

Army Form C. 2118.

Place	Date	Hour	Summary of Events and Information	Remarks and references to Appendices
	17/9/18		to get in touch with the enemy in order to locate his M.G. positions. Operation was successful. The 11th Cameron Highlanders relieved the 10th K.O.S.B. in the line on the night of the 16/17th. The 10th K.O.S.B. moved down to Reserve Area.	JJR
	18/9/18		Bath in reserve from B19 a 3.4 to B25 d 2.3. B.H.Q. at LETT Fm. about B25 c 8.6.	JJR
	19/9/18		Enemy artillery active in vicinity of LETT Fm. 15 casualties.	JJR
			Situation unchanged. On the night of the 19th/20th the 10th K.O.S.B. relieved the 15th K.O.Y.L.I. in the support line (units 2 Corps in front line).	JJR
	20/9/18		Disposition: B.H.Q. at HOLLEBEQUE Fm. B20 c 4.7. E & F Coys in front line. E Coy. (H.Q. at B27 a 8.2) from B25 c 30. WIGAN POST. LIVERPOOL POST to JESUS Fm. F Coy. (H.Q. signal Box B28 b 27) from B25 c 80 to B28 c 30. "G" Coy. (H.Q. B22 c 5.4) in trenches at B16 c 10 (Support) "P" Coy. (H.Q. at T.I.B Fm B26 b 79) 3 platoons in vicinity of Coy. H.Q. One platoon in support to E Coy on SKIN FLINT Fm B27 d 7.0.	JJR
	21/9/18		Situation unchanged. Enemy M.G.s active at night.	JJR
	22/9/18		Heavy concentration of enemy 5.9s in vicinity of HOLLEBEQUE Fm (B.H.Q.)	JJR

Army Form C. 2118.

10th BATTALION,
KING'S OWN
SCOTTISH BORDERERS.

No.
Date.

WAR DIARY
or
INTELLIGENCE SUMMARY.
(Erase heading not required.)

Volume IV Page III

Instructions regarding War Diaries and Intelligence Summaries are contained in F. S. Regs., Part II and the Staff Manual respectively. Title pages will be prepared in manuscript.

Place	Date	Hour	Summary of Events and Information	Remarks and references to Appendices
	22/8		Working Parties (10R 30-0R5) detailed for work on posts in vicinity of PONT de NIEPPE.	9/B
	23/8 9/8		On the night of the 23/24th the 10th KOSB were relieved by 8th R.I.R. The 10th KOSB moved back to LE GRAND BEAUMART A>K.	9/R
	24/8 to 30/8		Brigade in Divisional Reserve. Battalion training.	9/R

A.R. Rowland Lt
for Lt Col
Comdg
10th KOSB

WAR DIARY or INTELLIGENCE SUMMARY

October 1918
Vol I
10th K.O.S.B.

Place	Date	Hour	Summary of Events and Information	Remarks and references to Appendices
Sheet 26 new Grand at Beaumont Ha.	1		The Battalion advanced from Grand Beaumont at 7 pm. "B" Companies occupying posts along the Lys, "A" D Coys in reserve near Sergent Funeraires. H.Qrs at Regent Farm, relieving the 2nd P.S. Regt.	OAR
Egnynghem	2		During the afternoon "B" Coy and one platoon of "D" Coy crossed the Lys at Gospel Villa and took up a position near Egnynghem Switch.	OAR
	3		The Battalion advanced at dawn. "D" Coy on the left (passing through "B" Coy). "C" Coy on the right occupying the old British Reserve Line near Chapelle d'Armentières. Forward H.Qrs at Rue Maele. Rear H.Q. Epinette	OAR
	4		At dawn "B" Coy relieved "C" Coy. "C" returning to Rue Maele & supplying posts along the railway to prevent ingress into Armentières which was out of bounds. "D" Coy moved forward & occupied posts near & to the right of the railway crossing. "B" attacked them on their former position.	OAR
	5		"B" Coy advanced to the old British support trenches in Central Avenue & managed to get in touch with the 119 Bde on the left.	OAR
	6		"C" Coy was ordered to advance to the old German front line & endeavour	

WAR DIARY / INTELLIGENCE SUMMARY

Army Form C. 2118.

Volume I
October 1918.
10/K.O.S.B

Page 26

Place	Date	Hour	Summary of Events and Information	Remarks and references to Appendices
Sheet 36 1/20,000	6th		Trench but was held up by M.G's and remained in occupation of the Old British Front line trenches near Central Avenue. The Battalion was relieved by the 11" Camerons that night returning "C" Coy to Eeywenhem Church, A'73 to the factory & rest to Ependate.	
	9th	9 o'clock	Battalion in Brigade Reserve about Ergenwhem.	
		10 o'c	Having relieved 11" Camerons in support on night of 9". Battalion takes "B" Coy holding at Rue Marle. "A" Coy in Chappelle D'Amentieres. "D" Coy in 4 posts, West side of Lys from 65e50 to 621 Central. "C" Coy in Asylum at 12a22. Holding posts from 12c68 to 12t4.3. "D" Coy holding posts on West side of Lys from 620d.3.7 to 621c.12 On morning of 12 inst attached (through Camerons) barnate Trench and gained about 800 yards of same, and were relieved same night by a company of 11" Camerons. They then returned to support lines.	
	13th		Night of 13" Battalion were relieved by 23 Bn Lancs Fusiliers	

Page 2

WAR DIARY
or
INTELLIGENCE SUMMARY.

Volume I
October 1918
10th K.O.S.B.

Army Form C. 2118.

Place	Date	Hour	Summary of Events and Information	Remarks and references to Appendices
Pont de Nieppe	13		and returned to Pont de Nieppe	
	14		Brigade in Divl Support. Battalion in training	
	15		Shelling Nieppe dugouts	O.T.R.
sheet 36 N.40.c.0.0	16		Moved by march route via L Bizet to Armentieres & Houplines	O.T.R.
	17		" " " to Croix du Bac	O.T.R.
	18		" " " Wambrechies	O.T.R.
	19		" " " St. Andre	O.T.R.
St Andre	20		O/O Brigade in Divl Battalion in training and working on railway	O.T.R.
sheet 37 N.00.0.0.0	27		Moved by march route to Lannoy	O.T.R.
Lannoy	28			O.T.R.
	29 to 31		Battalion in training (Brigade in Divisional Reserve)	O.T.R.

M. Anderson
Lt Col
COMDG. 10th K.O.S.B.

WAR DIARY
INTELLIGENCE SUMMARY

NOVEMBER 1918.
VOLUME I. Page 28.
10TH K.O.S.B.
Army Form C. 2118.

Place	Date	Hour	Summary of Events and Information	Remarks and references to Appendices
LANNOY	1st		Battalion in training. Lewis Gun, & Signalling classes.	R.S.
"	2nd		" " Classes as usual.	R.S.
"	3rd		" Church Parade.	R.S.
"	4th		" in training. Bachs.	R.S.
"	5th		" "	R.S.
"	6th		" Lewis Gun Class.	R.S.
LEERS NORD	7th		Battalion relieved 2/3rd Cheshire Regt in the support area, marching via FRESNOY - LEERS to LEERS NORD. Battalion in training. Signalling & bombing classes. Major. S. Boyd. M.C. assumed command of Battalion vice Lt. Col. M. Archer-Shee. D.S.O. to England.	R.S.
"	8th		Battalion in training. Lewis Gun Signalling & Bombing classes. Revolver class for Nos 1 & 2 Lewis Gunners.	R.S.
"	9th		Moved via march route to new billets in PECQ area.	R.S.
PECQ	10th		Battalion Church Parade. March to new billets in HERINNES. Working parties on roads at PECQ.	R.S.
HERINNES	11th		Battalion in training. Working party repairing bridge.	R.S.

NOVEMBER 1918 VOLUME I
Page 29
10TH K.O.S.B.

WAR DIARY
or
INTELLIGENCE SUMMARY.

Army Form C. 2118.

Place	Date	Hour	Summary of Events and Information	Remarks and references to Appendices
HERINNES	12TH		Moved by march route via LE RIVAGE - PECQ - H11 central - NECHIN to TOUFFLERS	R.S.
TOUFFLERS	13TH		Battalion in training.	R.S.
"	14TH		" " " Recreational training	R.S.
"	15TH		Rehearsal of Brigade Ceremonial parade at G.30.C. central. Major T.J. Gough M.C. reported for duty as 2nd in command on 14/11/18 from 13TH BN EAST LANCS REGT.	R.S.
"	16TH		Brigade route march	R.S.
"	17TH		Battalion church parades	R.S.
"	18TH		Battalion in training	R.S.
"	19TH		Inspection of Battalion by Corps Commander at H.14.d.	R.S.
"	20TH		Battalion in training	R.S.
"	21ST		" " " " Baths	R.S.
"	22ND		" " " "	R.S.
"	23RD		" " " "	R.S.

NOVEMBER 1918.

VOLUME I
Page 30.
10TH K.O.S.B

WAR DIARY
or
INTELLIGENCE SUMMARY.

Army Form C. 2118.

(Erase heading not required.)

Place	Date	Hour	Summary of Events and Information	Remarks and references to Appendices
HERINNES	24th		Battalion Church Parades	R.S.
"	25th		Battalion in training	R.S.
"	26th		" " " Route march.	R.S.
"	27th		" " " "	R.S.
"	28th		" " " "	R.S.
"	29th		Inspection of D. Coy. by G.O.C.	R.S.
"	30th		Battalion in training & Baths	R.S.

S. Baxter
Lt.-Col.
Comdg. 10th K.O.S.B.

December 1917
Volume I
Page 31.
10th Bn K.O.S.B

WAR DIARY OF INTELLIGENCE SUMMARY.

Army Form C. 2118.

Place	Date	Hour	Summary of Events and Information	Remarks and references to Appendices
TOUFFLERS	1st/12/18		Battalion Church Parades	RS
"	2nd		" in Training, Route March, Recreational Training	RS
"	3rd		Inspection of "A" Coy by G.O.C. Recreational Training	RS
"	4th		Probe Ceremonie Prise at NECHIN (H.14.d.)	RS
"	5th		Battalion in Training. Inspection of "C" Coy by C.O. Recreational Training	RS
"	6th		" (Bn dispatched 35 NCOs & 85 men = 9 offs + N.G.s) Inspection of "C" Coy by C.O. Recreation	RS
"	7th		Battalion Inspection by C.O. Bn football team defeated 11th Bn Cameron Highrs (by 2 goals to nil)	RS
"	8th		Battalion Church Parades. Recreation	RS
"	9th		Battalion in Training. Inspection of "C" Coy by G.O.C. by Divl Cmdr.	RS
"	10th		" Recreational Training	RS
"	11th		" Recreational Training	RS
"	12th		Inspection of "B" Coy by C.O. Recreational Training	RS
"	13th		" Recreational Training	RS
"	14th		" Baths	RS
"	15th		Battalion Church Parades.	RS
"	16th		" Route March. Recreational Training	RS

Army Form C. 2118.

WAR DIARY
or
INTELLIGENCE SUMMARY.

(Erase heading not required.)

December 1918. Volume I. Page 32.
10th Bn KOSB

Place	Date	Hour	Summary of Events and Information	Remarks and references to Appendices
TOUFFLERS	17/12/18		Divisional Ceremonial Parade at NECHIN (X.14.d.)	R.S.
"	18th		Battalion in Training. Inspection of men & Billets by M.O.	R.S.
"	19th		" Recreational Training	R.S.
			Recreational Training (Football Semi Final) Bn represented R.A.M.C. by 2 G.H.Z.	
"	20th		Battalion Route March. Recreational Training	R.S.
"	21st		Battalion Inspection by C.O. D Coy on Range	R.S.
"	22nd		Battalion Church Parade. Route March Reconnaissance Training	R.S.
"	23rd		" Training	R.S.
"	24th		" "	R.S.
"	25th		Battalion Church Parades.	R.S.
"	26th		No Parades	R.S.
"	27th		Battalion in Training & Baths	R.S.
"	28th		" Inspection by C.O. & Route Parades	R.S.
"	29th		" Training. Football Game. Bn defeated 178 Bde R.F.A. by 2.6.1	R.S.
"	30th		" Cleaning Equipment & Billets Medals presented by Major General	R.S.
"	31st			R.S.

S. Boyle

January 1919
Volume 1
Page 33
Army Form C. 2118.

10th Batt: S.O.S.B. F9F

WAR DIARY
or
INTELLIGENCE SUMMARY.
(Erase heading not required)

Instructions regarding War Diaries and Intelligence Summaries are contained in F. S. Regs., Part II. and the Staff Manual respectively. Title pages will be prepared in manuscript.

Vol 8

Place	Date	Hour	Summary of Events and Information	Remarks and references to Appendices
Soufflens	1st		Batt: in training, musketry, Bayonet Drill & Physical Training	45.
	2nd		Bayonet Training, Bayonet Drill, Marching & Range Duties	45.
	3rd		Batt: + A Coy. on Range Duties	45.
	4th		Batt: inspection by C.O. & Cross Country Run	45.
	5th		Church Parade	45.
	6th		Batt: Inspection, musketry & Bayonet drill	45.
			Major J.T. Bruges M.C. proceeded on leave 2nd Army Command	
	7th		Inspection by Divisional Commander	45.
	8th		Batt: Parade, Brade Circuit close order & Coy.	45.
	9th		Ceremonial Parade	45.
	10th		Batt: 2 and ½ sec of ¾ chapel & Coy, Gordon Guard, practice to assemblage & Colours	45.
	11th		Batt: Inspection by C.O. Lothtel Batt: in opening parade of 39th MG Corps Batt: MGC 5th Gds: to Ni	45.
	12th		Batt: Church Parade	45.
	13th		Practice Ceremonial Parade & Presentation of Colours at Tonbrise	45.
	14th		Batt: Drill, Football match between A + B Coys	45.
	15th		Ceremonial Parade & Presentation of Colours at Tonbrise	45.
	16th		Practice Reconnaissance Route march	45.
	17th		Ceremonial Parade for review & Presentation of Colours the Duke of Lancy.	45.
	18th		Lille Ceremonial Review for Presentation of Colours.	45.
	19th		Batt: Church Parade	45.
	20th		Presentation & Presentation of Colours of C.2.C.9.6. by XV Corps Comdr.	45.
	21st		Lord Guard Sir Beauvoir de Lisle K.C.B. D.S.O.	45.
			Batt: Ceremonial Parade.	
			Batt: Parade and Vac of Officers Photographs.	
	22nd		Range allotted to D Coy A.B.C. Musketry Physical Training & Company Drill	45.

Army Form C. 2118.

Volume 1
Page 34
10th Batt K.O.S.B.

January 1919

WAR DIARY
or
INTELLIGENCE SUMMARY.
(Erase heading not required.)

Instructions regarding War Diaries and Intelligence Summaries are contained in F. S. Regs., Part II. and the Staff Manual respectively. Title pages will be prepared in manuscript.

Place	Date	Hour	Summary of Events and Information	Remarks and references to Appendices
Tuffeins	23rd		Battn Parade & Visit of Official Photographers. Lt Col returned from leave.	605
	24th		Baths at Camery & disposal	605
	25th		Att inspection, Cleaning of Billets. C° Condrs	605
	26th		Battn Wheel Parade & C° Coy on Range	605
	27th		Baths & disposal & C° Condrs	605
	28th		C° Condrs inspection & Training	605
	29th		C° Condrs Inspection & disposal Major J T Gough MC succeeded on leave to UK	605
	30th		C° Condrs inspection & disposal	605
	31st		C° Condrs Inspection & disposal	605

1/2/19

S. Boyle
Lt Col Comdg
10/16 O.S.B.

WAR DIARY or INTELLIGENCE SUMMARY

February 1919 — Volume I — Army Form C. 2118

Page 34

Place	Date	Hour	Summary of Events and Information	Remarks and references to Appendices
TOUFFLERS	1.2.19	07.30	Breakfast Drill O.R. 09.00 hrs Coy Comdrs inspection. Physical — Ammo Drill	
"	2.2.19	"	Blanket Shaking 10.05 in Parisian Sanitare Barracks (B/E, B Coy Phd.)	
"	3.2.19	"	Inspection of Greatcoats 09.00 hrs Coy Comdrs inspection	
"	4.2.19	"	Whole Kit Brown Paper 09.00 hrs 12.30 hrs parade & take at ROUBAIX	
"	5.2.19	"	Mess Tins 09.00 hrs Coy Comdrs Inspection & Coys at disposal of Coy Comdrs	
"	6.2.19	"	Towels — 09.00 hrs Coy Comdrs inspection. Recreation — Ammo Drill	
"	7.2.19	"	ENTRENCHING TOOL HELVES. 09.00 hrs Inspection by Coy Comdrs. Rifle Inspection & Cmds shoot	
"	8.2.19	"	HOLDALL 09.00 hrs inspection. Lecture by Medical Officer & Educational training	
"	9.2.19	"	BLANKET SHAKING. C&E. R.C. — Pres Brodie	
"	10.2.19	"	Inspection of FANS 09.00 Coy Comdrs inspection Educational training	
"	11.2.19	"	HAVERSACKS. Coy Bomdrs inspection 09.00 hrs Ammo Drills — Educational training	
"	12.2.19	"	BELTS. 09.30 hrs inspection Educational training 2.45 march to Stake & ROUBAIX	
"	13.2.19	"	BRACES, WATER BOTTLES + CARRIERS 09.00 hrs Coy Comdrs inspection — Physical training	
"	14.2.19	"	ENTRENCHING TOOL + CARRIER 4 Coy Cmdrs inspection 09.00 hrs + Ammo drill	
"	15.2.19	"	BAYONET SCABBARD + FROG 10.00 hrs Comdg Officers inspection 11.00 hrs Educational training	

WAR DIARY or INTELLIGENCE SUMMARY

Army Form C. 2118.

February 1919   Volume 1   Page 35

10 Battn KOSB

Place	Date	Hour	Summary of Events and Information	Remarks and references to Appendices
TOUFFLERS	16.2.19	07.30	BLANKET SHAKING & INSPECTION. 6.15 R.C. - Pres. parade	SH
"	17.2.19	"	Inspection of Box Respirator. 09.00 Coy. Officers inspection. Aims Drill + Educational training	SH
"	18.2.19	"	RIFLE SLING 09.00 hrs. Battalion Parade and inspection. Arms drill etc.	SH
"	19.2.19	"	GREATCOATS 09.00 inspection by Coy Comdr. Reprisal of Educational training	SH
"	20.2.19	"	KNIFE FORK, SPOON + RAZOR 09.00 Inspection by Coy Comdr. 12.45 March K. Baths at ROUBAIX	SH
"	21.2.19	"	MESS TIN Inspection by Coy Comdo 09.00 hrs. Reprisal + Arms Drill, Inspection of Rifles by Coy Officers	SH
"	22.2.19	"	TOWELS Battalion Parade 09.15 Inspection by Com'd'g Officer and arms drill	SH
"	23.2.19	"	BLANKET SHAKING. Parade Service in C/E, R.C. + PRES.	SH
"	24.2.19	"	Inspection of ENTRENCHING TOOL HELVES 09.00 Inspection by Coy Comdr. 10.30 Educational training	SH
"	25.2.19	"	HOLDALL inspection by Coy comdr at 09.00 Arms drill + Physical training	SH
"	26.2.19	"	PACKS. 09.00 hrs Coy Comdr inspection Lecture + Educational training	SH
"	27.2.19	"	HAVERSACKS 09.00 hrs coy Comdr inspection and coy training of his disposal	SH
"	28.2.19	"	BELTS 09.00 " Coy Comdr inspection Comdg officer roll inspect Kilts	SH

Major
O.C. 10.K.O.S.B

www.ingramcontent.com/pod-product-compliance
Lightning Source LLC
Chambersburg PA
CBHW081248170426
43191CB00037B/2082